AMBASSADORS JOURNEY

MAXO DEJANIS

Order this book online at www.trafford.com
or email orders@trafford.com

Most Trafford titles are also available at major online book retailers.

Print information available on the last page.

ISBN: 978-1-4907-6984-4 (sc)
ISBN: 978-1-4907-6983-7 (e)

Trafford rev. 06/16/2016

www.trafford.com
North America & international
toll-free: 1 888 232 4444 (USA & Canada)
fax: 812 355 4082

DEDICATION

This book is dedicated, first of all, to God, and to our Lord Jesus Christ of Nazareth.

Secondly, I would like to dedicate it to my family and friends, especially my loving wife Marline Dejanis, my daughters Dejuana and Marlina, and my goddaughter Lenora James; also to my older sister Liliane, and my brothers Mario, Jerry, and Steve; to my prayer partner and mentor, Jonathan English, his wife SueEllen, and their children Hannah and Rachel; to my brother Samuel, his wife Elisabeth, and their children Victoria and Isabelle.

I would also like to express my appreciation to all our church members and pastors who have been with us and are still with us—you are all so valuable to me! My thanks to David Keeler for his help with editing this book. And may God use this book to reach many who are as yet unsaved!

INTRODUCTION

" Let the peace of Christ rule in your hearts, since as members of one body you were called to peace. And be thankful. Colossians 3:15

I have much to be thankful for! With God's blessings upon me, I have lived half a century. I am in good health and physically fit, and I don't even look 50 years old!

God has also blessed me with a wonderful wife—my number one prayer partner. She has seen me as a husband, a father, and a preacher in both triumph and failure. She has been there for me in my struggles, even when I have been fearful or depressed. She has witnessed miracles of God's redemption, as He brings forth gold from the ashes. Every step of my journey, I have been accompanied by her prayers.

I have written this book to share my experiences in the ministry over the years. To be an ambassador for Christ is a noble calling. There may be challenges involved, but by God's grace, we will always be victorious. It is God that calls us. He welcomes us into the high privilege of talking with Him and working with Him.

As you read this book, my prayer is that it will lead you into your own call for ministry, will help you build a stronger relationship with God, and help you to build your own altar at home, in your community, reaching out to every part of the world. All of us are called to tell the world that Jesus is alive and active today, to preach, and to teach. Enjoy your reading, and feel free to share what you learn from this book. May God bless you all.

MINISTRY EXPERIENCE— MAXO'S CALL TO JAMAICA

I n 1990, I had just finished my course work in Haiti, in the field of mass communication. Having invested a great deal in my education, my father expected me to continue my schooling, moving on to the study of general medicine. When I told him that I had been called to go to Bible school in Jamaica, my father was very upset. He could not understand why I would waste all the time and energy I had spent on my education, as well as all the money he had invested in me. Finally, he turned his back on me, but I refused to give up my calling. I remember telling him that I would find a way to attend Bible school, and one day I would return to Haiti and start a church, a school, a health center, and a radio station. He just laughed at me and walked away, but I would not allow anything to stop me from pursuing my dream, large as it was.

As I had not a cent to my name, I knew I would need a miracle from God. Soon, my father was visited by a friend from Miami; months later, the friend sent his girlfriend to spend a week in Haiti. She needed a translator in French-speaking Haiti, and he thought I would be just the one to help her. I didn't know much

English, so I bought an English dictionary and studied hard before her arrival. I became a successful translator for her!

She had a video camera, and I helped her to document her entire trip. In exchange, she gave me the camera when she left Haiti. I was able to sell the camera for $300.00, and purchased my ticket to Jamaica!

But the Bible school in Jamaica did not want to accept me. I did not speak English. I had not waited for a proper letter of acceptance before arriving. And, since I had only enough money for a one-way ticket to Jamaica, I had not fulfilled the school's requirement (for immigration purposes) of a two- way ticket. Unfortunately, I got the school management into trouble with immigration, and they said the only solution was to send me back to Haiti.

I remained steadfast in the promise that he whom God blesses, no man can curse! God knew that the week I left Haiti, serious political problems developed there. The school tried many times to book me on a flight to Haiti, but, because of the political atmosphere, no planes were allowed to land there. In fact, the flight on which I arrived in Jamaica never returned to Haiti. Miraculously, I had been able to leave Haiti before the problems developed, and God used them to keep me in Jamaica.

I will never forget the day I found myself in the schoolyard, working with a rake and a wheelbarrow to earn my food and shelter. I was not a student, but I could not be sent back to my homeland, and they didn't know what else to do with me. One day, the headmaster called for me. He told me that they knew God loved me. They had tried many ways to send me home, but none had worked. Therefore, they had no choice but to officially make me a student! I told him that I knew my God would not fail me.

An anonymous Canadian missionary paid for a year of Bible school for me. God is so good! When He calls you, He makes provision for you! I started out with only $300, but God had multiplied it for me. When I graduated, the school offered me a position, working on staff. Every day, I counted my blessings, as I waited for God to move me towards His vision for my life.

God will always accomplish His vision for each one of our lives. If we trust Him, He will always provide. Every day with Him is a new day, new and exciting!

My High School Story

Like most other boys leaving primary school and moving on to high school, I felt like a real man. I started to discover how attractive I was to the young girls. They see us as smart and handsome, with nice hairdos, and perfect chocolate complexions. They notice when we are always clean, but especially when we become the stars in the school! We start thinking about what looks and qualities we want in a girl who will become our wife, and to pick and choose our favorites from the girls in school.

I remember one young lady in particular. She seemed to admire me, but every time we met, she could not remember my name. She would always ask me if I could remind her what my name was. I'm afraid I was quite rude to her, saying, "I will tell you my name once and for all!" I made a joke out of it, saying, "Open your hand, and you will see my name written in the middle of it."

"No," she replied, "that cannot be!"

"I will prove it to you," I replied, "in the middle of your hand you will find M..A..X..O."

As I spoke, she took out a pen and started to mark out the letters in her hand. She smiled at me, and I told her, "Any time you look at the middle of your hand, you will always remember my name, because it is written in your hand. Even when you die, you will die with my name in your hand. But if you have Jesus, when you die, His Name will be in your heart forever!"

I want to give you a special invitation to a Man Who always cares about everyone. Listen to what He says in His Word.

"All have sinned, and fallen short of the Glory of God." Romans 3:23

"The wages of sin is death, but the free gift of God is eternal life in Jesus Christ our Lord." Romans 6:23

"But God demonstrated His love toward us, in that, while we were still sinners, Christ died for us." Romans 5:8

"By grace you have been saved through faith, and that not of yourselves; it is the gift of God, not of works, so that no one may boast." Ephesians 2:8-9

"If you confess with your mouth Jesus as Lord, and believe in your heart that God has raised Him from the dead, you will be saved." Romans 10:9-10

Here is a prayer you can pray; Jesus will hear you. "Lord Jesus, I realize that You died for me, so that I can be free today. Please, come into my heart. In the Name of Jesus of Nazareth, Amen. Amen and Amen."

MINISTRY EXPERIENCE
MARLENE'S TESTIMONY

I was born on the beautiful Caribbean Island of Jamaica, the land of wood and water. Although it is not well known, Jamaica gave refuge to some of the Jewish people who fled from Europe after World War II.

My mother gave birth to me in the beautiful parish of St. Ann, well known in Jamaica for being the home town of some of our most famous people. I was blessed to grow up in a Christian home; even my birth was a miracle.

My mother was dating my father when she was only sixteen years old. When she became pregnant, her family was greatly upset and soon made it clear that she was no longer welcome in their home. My father was unable to provide a home for her, and her mother even advised her to have an abortion. But my mother did not believe in abortion; instead, she trusted God to provide for her. She slept on peoples' porches throughout her pregnancy. In spite of the fact that all her dreams were shattered, she refused to give in to discouragement, and, instead, kept moving from door to door. At one time, one of her family members pushed a fish gun up against her belly, threatening to kill her because of her pregnancy. But God spared her life and mine, and, five months later, my mother gave birth to me in a hospital.

After leaving the hospital with me, my mother had no place to go. She went back to sleeping on the streets, and behind peoples' houses. After six months, my father's aunt took us to live with her in Portland, Jamaica. But two years later, without notice, my mother and I had to leave again. My uncle had a bitter quarrel with one of my cousins, a fight so savage that he actually bit his ear off. My mother was forced to flee back to St. Ann with me.

With nowhere else to go, she took me to the house of my father's dad. But he would not accept her; he held me upside down and threatened to cut me in two with the machete he held in his other hand. Many people were watching, when, by the providence of God, one of my cousins appeared out of nowhere and snatched me away from my grandfather. Fleeing the scene, he took me to the home of an old lady who lived next door, informing my father of my whereabouts. We were able to live with this lady for a few months, and she was the one who later told me the story of that terrible day.

My father was still in touch with my mother. He was able to get a job in construction and eventually, he was able to provide a one-room rental for the three of us. My father and mother had three more children together. After five years, my father was able to get a job in Canada picking apples, as well as a job cutting sugar cane. He travelled back and forth two or three times, bringing money to us. But eventually, he left and never came back. He did send money to us sporadically, but, due to his status as an illegal resident, he was constantly avoiding the police and his support was, to say the least, inconsistent. My mother was forced to play the role of both father and mother, and I, as the eldest child, inherited a great deal of responsibility.

In spite of opposition from other family members, my father had promised my mother that he would marry her one day. But the day came when he called my mother and told her he was going to marry another lady he had met. He broke my mother's heart.

One day, my mother sent me many miles away to get the mail. There was an air mail letter for my mother, and I was so happy that I ran home and handed it to her. I can still see her smile of happiness at receiving the letter. I was stunned when, five minutes later, she became cold and began to bleed heavily. She could not explain what was happening, but told us to read the letter. It said, "Kiss your loved ones; you have only four days to live." We took her to a pastor, who prayed over her. God healed her, and anointed her for His service. God Himself is the only reason my mother is alive today.

Although my mother did not have much, she insisted that I attend church every Sunday. I had only one dress to wear for many years, but it was my favorite. The other kids teased me about it, but I wore it until it no longer fit; my mother could not afford another dress for me. At the age of twelve, still in that little dress, I stood in the church and gave my heart to Jesus.

I wanted to be baptized immediately, but my mother said I needed to learn more before I took that step. I heeded her instruction, and, although I could not be baptized right away, I remained a faithful member of the church. And, later on, I received my baptism. Since that day, God has always remained faithful. He gave me a loving daughter, and called me to the ministry.

Marline Meets Maxo

Since my father was never there for me, and my mother was at home with four children, I was forced to find a job in order to help my mother. I found a job, cleaning house for my aunt and uncle.

My dream had always been to serve in the military, but, due to financial problems, I was never able to. I graduated from high school in 1996, but was unable to enrol in a college or university, or even to join the military. I became discouraged after a time, and began to contemplate my future. I didn't want to keep doing this—working only for my family, and earning only enough income to buy some food for them. One day, I asked my aunty for money to attend college, but, fearing that I would be unable to pay her back, she refused me. Frustrated and upset, I quit my job and began hunting for work in Ocho Rios.

I did manage to get a job as a sales representative in the tourism industry. This upset my aunt, but that could not stop me from moving on with my life to expand my future. I began to help my mother and my siblings, but never forgot my dreams to join the military. Nor did I lose my hope or my faith. I continually prayed that God would bless me with a hard-working and understanding husband. I always wanted to have my own house, and car, and business.

One day, while I cooked outdoors over a wood fire, weighed down by the stress and burdens of my life, a vision came to me. I saw myself with a young man and three elderly missionaries, climbing a mountain in a strange land. I was perplexed by this vision, but understood that God was giving me a glimpse of His plan for my future.

While I was at work one day, three young men came into my office and greeted me. One of them, seeing how timid I was, got my phone number from one of my friends instead of asking me directly. Two weeks later, he called me. My mother asked who was calling, and I told her it was just a friend; but that wasn't enough for her. She wanted to meet the guy I was talking to, and give her approval before I could continue talking with him. Being a gentle man, Maxo gladly agreed to meet with her.

We would meet in the street, so the neighbors could keep an eye on me. My mother gave me a six o'clock curfew; Maxo always respected her wishes, and would bring me home on time. She had nothing bad to say about him, and actually was pleased with him and approved my being with him. And so a real relationship began to grow!

MINISTRY EXPERIENCE IN JAMAICA

Mile End is a little neighborhood in St. Ann, Jamaica, where Marline was born and raised. When I met Marline, I was living in Montego Bay, so I moved to Mile End in order to join her there. I did not have a church in which to worship, so I visited many churches all over the area. My focus was evangelism; I often watched evangelists on television.

One bright Sunday morning, I told my brother-in-law that I was going home. "Why would you go back to Haiti?" he asked.

"No," I replied. "I'm not returning to Haiti. I am going to church." I had been to church many times, but it had never meant that much to me. This day, my heart felt different. The Holy Spirit led me to a church in my neighborhood. Only three people were at the church that day, and I was asked to give my testimony. I did so, and that testimony became the preaching for the day.

Since there was no minister for that church, I began to lead the services. The church began to grow, and the community to come back together. The Lord's blessings began to flow out reaching many other places. I decided to start a pre-school, and, in only one day, I registered thirty students.

But the devil, hating to see God's Kingdom progressing, turned some of the church members against me. They were jealous of the rapid growth of the church and school, and did not want to see me leading both. I was responsible for the finances for the construction of the new school.

One day, the cook offered me some lunch, but I said no, I had already eaten. This went on several times, but I always refused the lunch the cook offered me. Then came the day when I was preaching, and one of the angry men from the community arrived in the church with rocks and a machete, planning to kill me in the pulpit. As he began to throw rocks at me, the seventy people in the congregation fled, leaving me alone with my wife and two-year-old daughter. My wife tried to shut the doors, but the attacker was moving too fast. So she pushed me into the bathroom, and closed the door. I didn't understand why I should hide, but she was insistent.

My assailant pushed Marline aside, and tried to open the bathroom door. "Before you can kill him, you will have to kill me and my baby!" she shouted at him. And then she cried out, 'Jesus of Nazareth, what is this?" She lost control of her bladder. The attacker saw the flood and said, "He is one lucky man!" and ran away. Marline was able to call for help and get us out of the church safely.

Since we knew the family of my would-be murderer, I advised Marline to visit him at his place of work the next day. Taking a co-worker, she went to see him. When she asked him what the problem was between him and her husband, he began to use foul language and revealed that they had been planning to poison me. How thankful I was that Marline had always been the one to prepare my lunch!

After this incident, I stopped mentoring the church, so as not to put our lives in danger. I heard the voice of the Lord saying, "Do not go back to that church. I have a better plan for you. Go back to your native land, in Haiti, and I will bless you there."

I was soon to discover that he whom God blesses, no man can curse!

MINISTRY BIRTH IN HAITI 2003

After I returned to my homeland in Haiti, I had the privilege of meeting many ministers and getting involved in different activities. I realized then that ministries are not only for the pulpit, but must be extended outside the four walls of the church. And it became clear that Haiti was in great need of ministry.

With my wife and my daughter Dejuana, I had arrived in Haiti with great expectations of starting a church, a school, and a health center. Actually, however, we did not have the money to even rent a place for us to stay. We stayed with my brother, and my sister supported us financially. She sent us food in barrels from Miami, so that we could survive.

One day a friend of my brother came to the house and saw me leading a Bible study in the living room. At the completion of the study, he asked me if I would be interested in buying a piece of land to fulfill my dream. I said that I didn't think I was ready for that yet.

I began leading Bible studies in a yard in the community, with a tarpaulin for shelter. Eventually, fifty people were coming to a service and Bible study every Wednesday night. That ministry gave birth to another church ministry in another town in Haiti.

We invited missionaries from Indiana in the US to preach the good news of Jesus Christ. One young man repeatedly asked me if I wanted a piece of land to buy.

I told him yes, and he took me to a place called Pernier and showed me some land for sale at six to seven thousand dollars per lot. I asked him why he would bring me there and show me that land when he knew that I did not have any money. Another pastor friend there with us noticed the fertile land in the community, and wanted to produce corn and beets there, but I was focused on my vision.

As we walked around the community, I saw an old lady sitting under a tree. She acknowledged us as we walked towards her, and asked who we were. "We are pastors," I replied.

She was delighted, and asked what brought us there. I told her I was looking for a piece of land on which to build a church, a school, and a health center. Pausing for a few moments, she asked me to repeat that. When I had done so, she pointed to a section of land and told me that it had been donated to a pastor by her family so that he could build a church there, but, after a while, the pastor had disappeared and could not be found. She asked me to leave a phone number. Thrilled, I told my friends that it looked like something was going to work out in my favor.

Two weeks later, the lady called and asked me to meet her at her house. I arrived to find the whole family assembled, and learned that all of them wanted to give me the land except the eldest brother, who wanted to meet me in person first. He was sick, and, since he was a voodoo priest, he did not believe in God. But when he met me, the Holy Spirit immediately ministered to him; he took me by the hand and led me to the middle of the land, asking me to have a word of prayer on the land, in the middle of the whole family and about fifty people who had gathered there.

After I had prayed, he told me that he 'washed his hands' of the land, and as of that day, the land belonged to me. I could do whatever I wanted with it, he said. I could choose anywhere on the land to build my house.

Two weeks after this, he died. God had kept him alive long enough to fulfill my vision. By God's grace, we now have a church and a school on that land. Many people from that village have been saved, and many delivered from demonic spirits. God is good all the time; and all the time, God is good!

Haiti Ministry Experience

A lot of negative things have been said about Haiti. Without trying to defend Haiti, or say that it is a good country, one thing I know is that we have more worshippers of Christ than any other Caribbean country. We have over ten million people, believers in Christ who take their faith very seriously. Haiti is the only place in the Caribbean you can start a ministry and in the space of two months have more people than you have seats for, so hungry are the people for the Word of God. The only problem we have is the language; French and Creole are so difficult to learn, that many missionaries do not want to take the challenge to learn, and as a result, they will not come to our country.

In 2006, my family and I faced another bad experience. We had come to our community as strangers, but with great visions. Our visions began to come to pass; we had an active school, employing more than one teacher, who, of course, expected to get a little salary at the end of each month.

One Friday morning, I went to the bank to withdraw some money for the payroll, as well as to do some other business. Without my knowing it, someone had followed me. I arrived home happy and relaxed, prepared to do my little payroll and then go to bed. As I usually did, I awoke in the middle of the night for prayer and returned to my bed. A few minutes later, we heard a voice calling for us to open the door.

"Who is it?" I asked, but the person outside continued to demand that I open up.

"Open it yourself, if you can," I responded, "But I will not." Suddenly a gunshot shattered my window.

"Get down on the ground!" I shouted to my family. The thieves outside began to come in through the damaged window and began demanding "Where is the money?"

"What money?" I answered.

"The money you got from the bank today," they replied, and began to overturn everything in the house. I was forced to the floor and my family into the bed. The only thing I could pray at that moment was "O God, let Your will be done!"

I began to argue with the thieves. "You've come to the wrong place," I told them. "If I did have money, I would leave this place. The reason I am staying is so that I can help this community."

One of the fifteen gunmen was inside the house, and said to the others 'Come on, let's move! Don't you see these people keep praying?" Everyone of them grabbed something from my house; one of them found my locked briefcase, but could not open it because he did not know the code. "I've got it!" he shouted. "Let's go!"

It was about 1:30 AM. I told my wife that we needed to get out of there, quickly. A sudden dark cloud covered the community, and, under cover of the darkness, we safely reached a neighbor's house. Having heard so many gunshots, everybody in the community thought we must have been killed or kidnapped. But our God is good! He did not give the thieves any authority to touch us, and so He kept us safe.

A few days later, we moved to the Dominican Republic for refuge. We began to serve in Duarte, preaching the Gospel in many churches. We received the opportunity to start a church there, as well as a chaplaincy ministry, gospel recording and interviews on a radio station. We felt at home, and our Dominican friends and Haitian friends did not want us to leave. "Pastor," they told me, "we have land you can use to build a church here." But I knew it was time for us to leave; God wanted us back in Jamaica, the beginning of a new season in our lives.

THE MAXO FAMILY RETURNS
TO JAMAICA—2007

Ministry and Miracles—our Experience

Our experiences in Haiti and Santo Domingo had been great, but certainly challenging at times. I learned there that not everyone likes it when you are doing well in the ministry. There are good people, but there are also bad apples!

Upon our return to Jamaica, we made the decision not to associate with any missionary's church. Don't take this the wrong way, but we had heard of problems in the Caribbean churches caused by affiliations with local and overseas churches—their problems could so easily become the problems of the new church. Local people always believed that the pastor could not be removed from the pulpit, because he had been hired by the overseas mission board.

While in Haiti and the Dominican Republic, I was introduced to chaplaincy ministry, and I was fascinated by the work—particularly in the Dominican Republic. In every police station, you could find a chaplain's desk. Adopting this idea, I decided that when I returned to Jamaica, I would start a chaplaincy ministry in the churches. But God had other plans for me.

Mission teams came to Jamaica from Indiana, and I was asked what my plans were. I told them "I love children. I will start a children's ministry, but I will not pastor a congregation."

"But we are here to tell you that we have a troubled church and a school in the Lime Hall district," they replied. "We believe you should take over both of them. Will you pray about this?"

My wife Marline did not want to go, so we did not. Besides, we had already decided we did not want to be a part of a mission church again! Our visitors said they would await our decision, and left the island.

But I could not escape the thought that the Lord wanted us to be there. Two days later, I met them at the church. I ended up taking the responsibility as pastor and overseer of Christ Community Church and School, and from that point onward, God began to bless us spiritually and physically. When we arrived, there were three people in the church; we have since witnessed ninety-five percent of the community receive baptism. We've enjoyed weddings together, and souls that have backslidden have returned home to God.

People have been delivered. One man, a retired police officer, had a stroke that partially paralyzed him. We laid hands on him, and God told me to tell him to get up. Immediately, God restored him; he jumped to his feet and ran!

There was a little baby who had a hole in her heart. Her mother took her to many different doctors, but she received no healing. Finally, she brought her to the church, and told me that her daughter was sick and the doctors had given up on her. I took the baby and prayed for her.

Next week, that mother took her baby for a doctor's visit. "Where did you take her?" asked the doctor. "What do you mean?" responded the mother. "She is healed," stated the doctor. The baby's mother then told him that she had brought her to the church, and her pastor had prayed for her. That baby is now a beautiful girl.

I have seen miracles of God in Limehall, and in different parts of Jamaica throughout my ministry. I have witnessed God's blessings on my life. I have travelled to many parts of the United States, and received awards, certificates, and an honorary doctorate in the ministry, as well as awards from the Jamaica constabulary force for the chaplaincy ministry. God has blessed us with a wonderful family in Canada, too, our "angels on earth."

I often look back and realize that all of this testimony began with three hundred dollars invested in the ministry. There have been many sacrifices made for the ministry; indeed, you will not succeed in ministry without a lot of determination. But one day, I will be able to leave a legacy to my child.

Pastor's wives have a special calling (Marline)

It requires a great deal of patient perseverance to be a pastor's wife, as well as understanding, loving, and caring; it also brings great joy and peace. As a ministry wife, I have learned to take the bad with the good, the criticism with the praise, the failures with the success. A pastor's wife in the West Indies faces even greater challenges, because of the great need of the people, especially financial need.

Every woman has different experiences in her own roles and responsibilities, and I believe that when one is called to be a ministry wife, God has called us for His own purposes. Sometimes, the church members want to see us as perfect, unable to make any mistakes; but we, too, are only flesh and blood. Like anyone else, we can make mistakes. Life as a ministry wife can be difficult at times, dealing with the ministry issues as well as our own personal issues. We walk a lonely road, sometimes. We might seek friendship in our church congregation, only to realize that we do not have someone we can trust completely with our stories. The wives of other pastors are sometimes too busy to listen to us or connect with us. We have a role as mentors, not just our husbands. We need other women intercessors we can connect with.

A pastor needs the support of his wife, not just of his congregation. My husband can get a lot of criticism after preaching a sermon; church members can feel like he is talking about their personal business. He needs someone, like me, to encourage him that he is doing a great job and preaching a powerful message.

Satan will try to sabotage your husband's ministry by destroying your marriage. Never let bitterness poison your soul. Be thankful; be forgiving. Build a fence around your marriage by the power of the Holy Spirit, and welcome a joyful spirit at all times.

Protect your children. Sadly, not everyone in the church loves them; they can be naturally jealous of the attention you give your children. Not everyone who comes to church is trustworthy, either. As you reach out to them and minister to them, make sure you do not put your own family at risk. For instance, do not invite anyone to spend the night in your home, unless you know them very well; you can still be helpful to them, but make different arrangements.

Get to know the ladies in your church; build relationships with them. Learn not to take offense easily. At times, you will be the teacher; at times, you will be the student, and must be open to learn from them. Teach them about faith, about hope, about love, and about being a good servant. Amen.

Marline Dejanis
Pastors wife

The Life of a Young Believer (Dejuana)

There are many challenges in the life of a young Christian. Many young people laugh at the idea, saying that the life of a Christian is a 'living hell' because there is no drinking or smoking, and, worst of all, no partying! All of us teenagers want to experience the teenage dream, partying, and shopping, hanging out with friends and having fun with your peers. Being a Christian does not mean you can't have fun, or go shopping, or hang out with your peers; we all come to a point where we need to loosen up and have fun with our peers. But we must always live life in a way that pleases God.

Being a Christian does not mean you must shut up your emotions toward society, or personal emotions towards a boy or a girl. What matters is how you handle these feelings. Of course Christians can date, as long as you have your parents' approval and you follow their guidelines! Dating is a necessary part of finding your soul mate. Many teenagers say that church boys and girls always wear loose and ugly clothing. This makes me laugh out loud! Every teenager has his or her own sense of fashion, and I know I love to look "rocking" in the latest fashion.

It's normal for a pastor's daughter to look good because everyone is watching you. You should dress well. We teens call it "looking hot." I wear pants, which many churches do not approve. Many churches do not approve of jewelry. Being a pastor's kid brings with it both advantages and disadvantages. We find we are the center of attraction wherever we go. We've been given a special gift from God to lead, and most of us have been given beautiful voices that touch people's hearts.

But there are disadvantages, too. Some people hate us for our blessings. Kids at school often pick on us because we are 'PK' (pastor's kids.) They say many negative things about us, but the truth is that they are jealous because we have been so blessed by

God. Hold your head high and let God lead you; He will give you a full life, beyond your dreams. Since the day I gave my life to God, I have been blessed and happy every single day of my life. So I encourage you to give your life to the Lord, be baptized, and maintain a healthy relationship with God.

Dejuana Maxiana Dejanis
Pastors Daughter

The Ambassador's Call

In 2 Corinthians 5:20, Paul says that Christians are ambassadors for Christ. He is not talking about someone who is just a church member, or goes to church, or claims to be a Christian. He is talking about believers, followers of Jesus, those who have accepted Christ, received water baptism and the baptism of the Holy Spirit, and are called to be ambassadors.

What is an ambassador? An ambassador is an official envoy who represents a foreign sovereign or a country, providing a relationship between the country that he lives in and the country he represents. An ambassador is appointed by the leadership of those he represents, and is given authority to speak on their behalf. What a powerful position that is! An ambassador can speak on behalf of his President—in other words, he functions as the President in the President's absence.

Paul says that he is an ambassador of the Kingdom of God. His work as an ambassador was to spread the message from his Ruler to the whole world he lived in. That message, he said, is reconciliation. We need the message of reconciliation in the world today; there is such a lack of love, forgiveness, patience, and understanding! We need a message of restoration.

Being an ambassador for Christ is of great importance from a Kingdom perspective. To follow Christ means to give up the kingdom of self and the kingdom of the world, and to pledge allegiance to the Kingdom of God. It means that our home is in Heaven, not on this earth. It is our responsibility to tell others about the Good News, so that they too can join the Kingdom of God.

An ambassador should live his life in the light of his identity in Christ. Our identity in Christ is, first and foremost, a new identity—we are new creations in Christ. Our new identity in Christ should be recognizable both to ourselves and to others.

We should be the same kind of people as Christ, for we are, quite literally, followers of Christ.

Ambassadors do, however, face difficulties

Anyone who tells you that committing your life to Christ will make your life easier is not telling you the whole truth. Sometimes, life may become more difficult after we come to Christ. The struggle against sin is more pronounced than before, and temptations never end. But if you fight the good fight, you will be victorious.

Leadership qualities of Ambassadors

Ambassadors need to recognize that leadership is the key to fulfilling visions and obtaining results.

An Ambassador is one who knows where he is going, and carries others along with him.

An Ambassador is developed, not discovered. Becoming an Ambassador is a process.

An Ambassador builds meaningful relationships with others.

Being an Ambassador means taking responsibility, not just holding an office.

An Ambassador moves his team towards its goal, enabling them to achieve that goal.

Characteristics of Ambassadors

Ambassadors are bold, visionary, committed, passionate, and focused. Ambassadors are both motivators and producers. We are moving towards the end of time, living in a season of faith. An Ambassador must believe that all things are possible with Christ. And an Ambassador will love people, even those he does not like.

Ambassadors must be able to hear the Voice of God

To hear the Voice of God, you must be a good friend of His. You will hear many voices speaking to you, when you need to make decisions, and not every voice you hear will be His Voice.

There is the Voice of God, and the voice of your conscience. There is the voice of reason. And there is the voice of your flesh, and the voice of the devil. Some of these voices will lead you in the opposite direction to the one pointed out by the Voice of God. The voice of the devil brings you fear. His voice will try to make you lose hope, or cause you to seek revenge for wrongs, or urge you not to forgive. His voice brings confusion and oppression, and will do all he can to blind your mind and cause you to disobey the Word of God.

In contrast, the Voice of God will guide you into the truth. His Voice will comfort you, exhort you, and remind you of His living and unchanging Word. His Voice will cause you to profit in Christ and increase your faith. His Voice will convict you of sin, and lead you to salvation. In all things, His Voice will build you up and cause you to triumph in life through Christ Jesus.

In order to hear the Voice of God, you must study His Word; you must spend time in prayer; and you must seek counsel from wise counsellors.

Ambassadors must love their enemies

Jesus said to love our enemies as we love ourselves. The most challenging command given by Jesus to those of us who are believers is to love our enemies-- someone who hates me, or persecutes me, or treats me spitefully, or stabs me in the back. We must love them even when they stop blessings from reaching us, or create divisions in our families, or even when they kill a family member. The natural response is "Love that person? NO WAY!!" But when Jesus says to love them, there is a reason.

What is love, really? Love is a sacrifice. Love is merciful. Love is faithful. Love is always giving. The Love of God is unconditional, blind to the faults of those who are loved. It takes over us, and we cannot control it. The Love of God ('Agape' in the Greek) is universal, a non-exclusive love for all of humanity. That is the Love God wants us to have; He tells us to love so that we can be like Him-- "Sons and daughters of your Father in Heaven", as He told His disciples, "Who makes His sun to rise on the evil and on the good, and sends His rain on the just and on the unjust." God loves the good and the bad; He knows that we, too, will meet both good and bad people in everyday life, and He wants our Love to be His Love, the same for everyone we meet.

He says in His word, "Love your enemies. Do good and lend, hoping for nothing in return; and your reward will be great." Remember that not everyone whom you love will return that love to you. However, you will also receive love, sometimes from the most unexpected people! So continue giving love, always and to all.

God tells us not to be overcome by evil, but to overcome evil with good. 'If your enemy is hungry," He says, "feed him. If he is thirsty, give him a drink; for in so doing, you will heap coals of fire on his head." This means that you will be teaching him how to love instead of hate. Your enemy can even become your good friend!

Sometimes, your worst enemy can be a family member; in fact, it is very difficult for someone who does not know you to become your enemy. If your son, for example, becomes your enemy, how will you deal with him. Hate him? NO! Rebuke the spirit that has come into him to make him hate you, and continue to love him as your son, from deep, deep within your heart. God sees your heart. When He tells us to love our enemies, He makes it possible for us to do so. Pray for your enemy, and ask God to win his heart.

Ambassadors must have a forgiving spirit.

If you do not know how to forgive, your ministry will never be successful.

If you do not know how to forgive, your life will be miserable. This is especially true if you have to meet the person you have not forgiven in your everyday life. Even if the person you have not forgiven has died, every time you remember them, you will feel guilty.

Jesus Christ, the Son of God (His Name alone is worthy of all worship!) forgave each one of us, so that we, in turn, can forgive our brethren. Paul wrote a letter to the Colossians, a letter which still speaks to us today, telling us about the character required in an ambassador. In the heart of an ambassador, there must be compassion, kindness, lowliness, meekness, and long suffering. We are to forgive others, believers and unbelievers alike. We are to forgive all offenses, even small differences of opinion, or thoughts, or unkind actions.

God expects us to forgive others in the same way we have been forgiven. Refusal to forgive will break our fellowship with God. Forgiveness is not a choice for an ambassador; it is a command. We must forgive if we want to be forgiven by God, or by those we have wronged. As ambassadors, we must reign in life by Christ Jesus, resisting all temptations to take revenge.

Unforgiveness leads to bondage; forgiveness leads to liberty. It's a wonderful feeling, knowing that you are not carrying the burden of a grudge in your heart. You will live in joy, with a smile on your face that brightens your whole surroundings.

Unforgiveness hurts only the victim, not the offender. If we, as the persons who were wronged, refuse to forgive, we will carry the hurt all the time. But if we will forgive the offender, our hurts will take wing and fly away. We will not be continually waiting for him to admit his guilt and ask forgiveness; that, in fact, may never happen. The important thing is to forgive the offender, publicly. Then, we will be free!

Remember how, in your childhood, you could simply forgive and move on? Remind yourself that you are forgiving others for the sake of your own soul, not because they even deserve forgiveness. Stop thinking over and over again of the bad things that happened in your past. Just let go-- don't struggle or try to force the issue. Simply forgive, truly and meaningfully. You may need to write out all your emotions so that you can release them.

Forgiveness does not mean that you forget the incident ever happened; it simply means that you have made the choice not to live in that incident forever. You are putting it behind you, and moving on into a brand new life. So forgive, forgive, forgive....

<u>You can become an ambassador, now</u>.

"It is appointed unto men once to die, and after that, the judgment." All of us will die one day-- whether rich or poor, good or bad, white or black. Each of us will face the judgment of a

Righteous God. And since each one of us is a sinner, each one of us needs to be saved. The prophet Isaiah, in Chapter 64:6 says that we have all become unclean; even our righteous acts are like filthy rags. We all shrivel up like a leaf, and our sins, like the wind, have swept us away.

You must start out on the right road. Repent, and be saved and baptized. Jesus set an example for us, being baptized by John. You cannot bring people to the throne of God if you are not an example to them yourself. Now that you are ready, what's next?

Are you called to serve others as an ambassador? Then offer spiritual guidance to individuals, deal with problems in your own home, at your work place. Expand outward to deal with issues in your community, and in your nation. Your job includes going to hospitals, schools, public markets, nursing homes and police stations. You will work in youth clubs, lead religious services, lead prayer sessions, and provide grief counselling.

You will have opportunity to connect with people from all different types of backgrounds. You must be trustworthy, able to maintain confidentiality. People will share sensitive information with you, and expect that you will keep it confidential.

People experience social and spiritual crisis on a daily basis. Be available to help, as much as you can, and be punctual! Study the Scriptures diligently, and get a degree. Become ordained by a religious organization, attend seminars and leadership training. Get a certification, a letter of recommendation, an ID badge, even a uniform to show you are an ambassador. Let your light shine in the darkness! Congratulations, and welcome to the family.

Now you can start a home church or a cell group. I can offer you training, with seminars and conferences on how to empower you as an ambassador. For more details, email me at mdejanis@yahoo.fr

Ambassador's prayer altar

When I am tested, I build an altar and speak with God. I ask Him my question, and God says "Come closer to Me. I want to open your eyes." He began to give me words, and I wrote songs. He opened doors so that I could go to a music studio and record my songs, in both Creole and English. Those songs are still a blessing in Haiti, being played nearly every day by a radio station.

God gave me a dream, repeated several times, to show me that Haiti was going to face a serious disaster. As I was in bed one night in 2003, in a dream I saw the people of Haiti, especially in the capital city of Port-au-Prince running from north to south crying "Jesus is coming!" When I looked at the sky, I saw scriptures written in many different colors, and the white house turned into a worship center. I did not understand the dream until 2010, when Haiti faced a powerful earthquake. The white house did indeed become a place of worship. This is the result of prayer at the altar.

I could go on and on with stories of my prayer altar, but I want to encourage you to build your own altar within yourself. In your challenging moments, do not listen to the negative people that surround you; you need people who can influence your life in a positive way. Be careful that you do not make a cross, or a bible, or the oil of anointing, or any other Christian item your altar. No, your heart is your altar, your heart and its relationship with God.

What is an altar? An altar can be a place that is designed or separated for the worship of God; a place to fellowship with God. It is a place where praise and prayer can be offered to God.

An altar symbolizes holiness. It is a place of refuge and comfort.

Your altar can be a family altar, a place where your family can meet to worship, pray, and fellowship. Or, your altar can be a church altar.

As you can see, the church itself is an altar. It serves as a unified place of worship for believers or individuals who come together to pour out their hearts to Jesus. You can have a corporate altar, where you invite many churches to come together for prayer and worship.

But the most important altar you must have is your personal altar, your quiet place; you should assign a time, committed and set aside for God to meet with you, one on one. It may be a specific time each day, in which you seek the Face of God through worship, praise, thanksgiving, and prayer. It can be any time during the day, when you stop and commune with God; He will always be there for you.

The Book of Psalms

The Book of Psalms is not just a book of songs and praises and worship; it is not just a Hymn book. But it is also a prayer book of the Bible.

The songs and prayers in the book of Psalms are composed by different authors over a long period of time. These songs and prayers were collected and used by the people of Israel in their worship and prayers. Eventually, this collection became the book of Psalms, included in the Jewish scriptures and, because it was canonized, it is accepted as God's Word. The book of Psalms contains words of prophesy. Some of these prophesies were fulfilled in the lives of Biblical characters such as Jesus or Judas; some of these prophesies have yet to be fulfilled. Some will be fulfilled in your life as you pray them.

The book of Psalms was used by Jesus, and quoted by many of the writers of the New Testament. It has been a treasured book of worship and prayer of the Christian Church since its beginning, and it will not stop being treasured in our own time.

Many needs have been met through the book of Psalms as they are used by God's people in worship and prayer.

As you read through the book of Psalms, you will discover specific ones that you will use in prayer, commanding instant results and answers to your prayers. As you receive these scriptural prescriptions, and use them in your personal or corporate devotions and prayers, I see that you will have rapid and instantaneous results following all your prayers, made in the Name of Jesus of Nazareth.

I strongly recommend that you use the Name of Jesus Christ after reading the psalms, closing with these words; "In the Name of the Father, the Son, and the Holy Spirit, now and forever, as it was from the beginning and will be unto the end, let Your Will be done, Amen! Amen, Amen."

Psalm 1

This Psalm shows the way to prosperity, even while still on this earth. It can be prayed for material blessings. It is also a prayer for a safe delivery for a pregnant woman.

Psalm 2

This Psalm can be prayed to avoid violence in families, communities, and even whole nations. It can be prayed for protection if you travel by sea, particularly in areas prone to tropical storms. Psalm 2 is also a good Psalm to read if you have a terrible headache.

Psalm 3

Pray this Psalm for protection from your enemy, and to renew your faith in God in the midst of certain circumstances. Psalm 3 is also a good Psalm to pray if you have a toothache or back pain.

Psalm 4

Read this Psalm if you need the presence of God. It can also be a prayer for a good harvest, whether you are a farmer or an entrepreneur.

Psalm 5

Psalm 5 is a prayer for help when people stand against you, rather than being with you. If you need motivation and strength, read this Psalm. Pray this Psalm for protection from criminals and thieves, or as a prayer for victory in a court of law. If you are unsuccessful in what you are doing, read this Psalm.

Psalm 6

Pray Psalm 6 if you are troubled by arthritis. This Psalm can also be a prayer for restored eyesight. Women can pray this Psalm when troubled by irregular periods. Pray this Psalm to renew your hope in God.

Psalm 7

Pray this Psalm for victory over evil spirits.

Psalm 8

Pray this Psalm to bring success into your life, or for protection from wild animals.

Psalm 9

This Psalm can be prayed for healing of children with serious illnesses, or a for the relief of poverty.

Psalm 10

Read this Psalm if you are under attack by an evil spirit.

Psalm 11
This Psalm helps you to overcome lying lips, and also to calm an aggressive personality.

Psalm 12
Psalm 12 will help you be free from bad influences. It can be prayed for healing from poor vision or blindness. Psalm 12 can be prayed for protection from sudden death, or to help you overcome anxiety and depression.

Psalm 13
Psalm 13 can be used to rebuke demonic forces. It is an effective prayer against temptation and corruption, and can be prayed for protection against heart attacks.

Psalm 14
Psalm 14 can be used as a prayer that others will love you.

Psalm 15
Psalm 15 can be used as a prayer for increased wisdom. It is also a prayer for the surety of your salvation, and can be prayed for healing of disabled children, or for healing of a high fever.

Psalm 16
Reading Psalm 16 when you are unhappy can restore joy to you. If your friends turn against you without reason, read this psalm. God can reveal the unknown to you through this psalm; it can also be prayed to prevent natural disasters or to reveal the presence of thieves in your midst.

Psalm 17
Psalm 17 can be prayed to prevent natural disasters. It can also be used as a prayer for safe travel.

Psalm 18

This psalm is a prayer for gifts, both natural and supernatural. Pray this psalm as you ask God for the Holy Spirit. It is good to read this psalm after you have recovered from an illness; indeed, it is a good prayer for deliverance from sickness, even when medication does no good for you.

Psalm 19

Psalm 19 can be used as a prayer for a safe delivery for a woman giving birth. It can also be prayed to cast out evil spirits.

Psalm 20

Psalm 20 is a psalm of thanksgiving. Read this psalm to pray for a calm mind, or if you need help in coping with the loss of a loved one.

Psalm 21

Psalm 21 can be used as a prayer against sickness, physical sicknesses like tuberculosis, anemia, or sinus infections, and even moral sickness. It can also be prayed when you are looking for promotion.

Psalm 22

Psalm 22 can be used as a prayer for material things and riches. It can be prayed against anything on earth that is troubling you.

Psalm 23

Read this psalm as a prayer for a clean heart, or as a prayer for protection against vanity. Pray through this psalm for revelation, or for dreams and visions to instruct you.

Psalm 24 and 25
Read and pray through these psalms for protection against the schemes of the enemy.

Psalm 26
If you are being blackmailed, this psalm can be used as a prayer for protection from imprisonment.

Psalm 27
Pray this psalm for protection if you are in a bad environment, or if you are receiving bad advice, or if danger is near. It can be prayed if you need hospitality in a foreign country.

Psalm 28
Pray this psalm in order to receive the fear of the Lord, or when you need to reconcile with your enemy.

Psalm 29
This psalm can be a prayer for enlarging your mind and spirit. This psalm is a particularly good prayer for senior citizens. It is a prayer for rooting out evil spirits.

Psalm 30
Psalm 30 can be prayed when you need the power of the Lord. It is also a prayer for protection against the worst traps.

Psalm 31
Psalm 31 is a prayer for forgiveness from God. It can also be prayed for healing, prevention of terminal illness, protection from disasters such as floods and landslides, and as a prayer for guidance in choosing your profession.

Psalm 32
This psalm is a prayer for grace and love

Psalm 33
Psalm 33 can be prayed for perseverance and patience. Pray this
psalm for protection of the lives of children, and to prevent famine
and misery.

Psalm 34
Pray this psalm for protection from persecution and the prevention
of poverty

Psalm 35
This psalm can be prayed as a rebuke to the enemy. You can also
pray this psalm for the protection of your livestock.

Psalm 36
This psalm can be prayed when you are trying to conceive, but are
unable. It can be prayed for protection of your health in all parts of
your body, and to receive material blessings.

Psalm 37
Pray this psalm when you need protection against all kinds of
illness—fevers, cancer, anemia—and even for protection against
weaknesses or addictions.

Psalm 38-39
Pray these psalms for protection against 'loose tongues'. They can
be prayed for protection against tragic death, or for knowing the
date of your own death. You can pray these psalms for the gift of
discernment, or of prophesy, or for other divine gifts.

Psalm 40

This psalm is a prayer of supplication for grace and protection, including protection from evil spirits. It is a favorite prayer for the poor and the mentally unstable.

Psalm 41-43

Pray these psalms for anyone who has lost hope. They can also be prayed for deliverance from wicked people, and for protection against other activity.

Psalm 44

Pray this psalm before a wedding, a prayer for a long and prosperous life.

Psalm 45-46

These psalms can be prayed for peace and unity. Use them as a prayer for a good relationship with the Lord and His Word. Pray them for victory over our enemy, and to restore peace between a wife and her husband.

Psalm 47

Pray this psalm for protection for your family and house against evil spirits, and for the love and respect of your friends.

Psalm 48

Pray this psalm when you are in need of humility. You can also pray this psalm when you want your enemies to fear you.

Psalm 49-50

These psalms are a prayer for protection against vicious criminals. They are also a prayer for forgiveness, and a plea for a pure life. You can also pray them for healing for someone with a fever.

Psalm 51
This psalm is a prayer for forgiveness of a serious sin. It can also be prayed for protection against traitors.

Psalm 52
This psalm can be prayed for prosperity, as well as for God's judgment against corruption and against those who fight against God.

Psalm 53-55
Pray these psalms to break the power of a curse. Reading these psalms daily will improve your memory and your intelligence. Psalms 52-55 are a prayer for victory over enemies, visible and invisible. You can also pray these psalms for adequate housing.

Psalm 56
Pray this psalm if you have lost hope, or you want to increase your confidence in God. It is also a prayer for relief from persecution or bullying from others.

Psalm 57
This is a psalm of thanks to God for His Glory and for His Love. It is a prayer for victory against black magic (obeah, voodoo, and witchcraft). It is also a prayer for protection from disaster, and for success in your business endeavors.

Psalm 58
Pray this psalm to overcome fear—fear of your enemy, fear of a gunman, fear of rape, and fear of wild animals.

Psalm 59
Pray this psalm for your country. It is also a prayer for someone who is demon possessed. If someone tells lies about you, read this psalm rather than seeking revenge.

Psalm 60
Pray this psalm for the government, the military, and for the police.

Psalm 61
Pray this psalm if you have lost something—your job or anything else. You can also pray this psalm for blessings on your house

Psalm 62
This psalm is a good prayer for the morning; you can pray this psalm to offer yourself to the Lord. Pray this psalm for a shower of rain in times of drought.

Psalm 63
Pray this psalm for protection against Satan. It can also be used as a prayer to overcome your fear of the night.

Psalm 64
Pray this psalm for protection of your livestock, such as goats or cows. It can also be a prayer for material blessings, and for protection against accidents. Pray this especially if your life has been threatened.

Psalm 65
Pray this psalm for someone who is seriously ill for a long period of time. It can also be used as a prayer for an abundant garden.

Psalm 66
This psalm can be prayed to cast out an evil spirit. You can also pray this psalm for an abundant garden.

Psalm 67-68

Pray these psalms for prosperity in your business. They can also be used as a prayer for recovery from a bad fever, and as a prayer for good health.

Psalm 69-70

Pray these psalms for protection—whether for children or adults. These psalms can be prayed for protection against flooding, and for relief from poverty. Faithfully praying these psalms can help you to reconcile with your enemy.

Psalm 71

Pray this psalm for the release of someone in prison who longs to be free. This psalm can also be a prayer to regain joy, even in old age.

Psalm 72

This psalm can be used as a prayer against poverty. It can also be prayed for healing of abdominal pain or heart troubles.

Psalm 73-83

These psalms can be prayed when someone accuses you. They can be used as a prayer for solutions to your problems, for success in a lawsuit, and for recovery from illness.

Psalm 84

If you are sick, and your condition deteriorates, pray this psalm.

Psalm 85

This psalm can be prayed for reconciliation with your friends. It can also be used as a prayer for your material needs.

Psalm 86-88

These psalms can be prayed for victory in your community. They can also be prayers for healing of serious sickness, or to avoiding sinning, or for safe travel.

Psalm 90

Read this psalm as a prayer for success in your work. It can also be prayed for protection from nightmares, to cast out evil spirits, and to be victorious in a house that has been a home to evil spirits.

Psalm 91

Pray this psalm for protection against bad accidents, for protection against evil spirits, and for protection of your sound mind.

Psalm 92

Pray this psalm if you wish to receive honor and riches. It can also be used as a prayer for inspiration and inventiveness, the wisdom to use what you have to maximum effect. If you are in need of good help, pray this psalm.

Psalm 93

Pray this psalm for healing of the eyes, the ears, or the feet. If you are facing a lawsuit, pray this psalm.

Psalm 94

This psalm can be prayed for freedom in case of kidnapping.

Psalm 95

Pray this psalm to bring your brothers or sisters to repentance.

Psalm 96-97

These psalms are a good prayer for keeping a family happy all the time.

Psalm 98
Pray this psalm to maintain peace and unity in your family.

Psalm 99
Pray this psalm to help you remain faithful to God

Psalm 100
This psalm can be prayed for victory over your enemies.

Psalm 101
Pray this psalm for relief from arthritis or heart malfunction. You can also pray it as a blessing or dedication for your baby. Pray this psalm for protection against evil spirits.

Psalm 102-103
These psalms can be prayed for healing for a woman who cannot conceive. They can also be used as a prayer for a good harvest, or to help you learn to love your daily work.

Psalm 104
Pray this psalm to ask God's favor for your business, to ask Him for health and prosperity, and for protection against any spirit that would disturb you.

Psalm 105-107
Pray these psalms to maintain your integrity. They can also be prayed for protection against famine, and for continued growth.

Psalm 108
This psalm is a prayer for success, in whatever you are doing.

Psalm 109
This psalm is a prayer for victory over your enemy.

Psalm 110-111

Pray these psalms to receive your friends, and to shun your enemies.

Psalm 112-113

Pray these psalms for protection of children, the weak, or others who need protection. You can also pray them for healing of the eyes, ears, mouth, hands, or feet.

Psalm 114

This psalm can be prayed for help in accomplishing what you have set out to do.

Psalm 115

This psalm is a prayer of thanks to the Lord.

Psalm 116

This psalm is a prayer for protection against sudden and violent death, such as a car crash or an airplane crash.

Psalm 117

This psalm is a prayer to God for deliverance from calamity.

Psalm 118

This can be prayed for humility and purity.

Psalm 119

With this psalm, you can pray for God to curse those who are cursing you.

Psalm 120

Pray this psalm for help if you are involved in a lawsuit.

Psalm 121
Psalm 121 is a good psalm to pray when you travel at night.

Psalm 122
This psalm can be used as a prayer for promotion to an honorable position

Psalm 123
This psalm can be prayed for healing for anemia.

Psalm 124
This psalm is a prayer for protection against traitors, and those who falsely pretend to be your friends.

Psalm 125
Pray this psalm for God's favor and protection for one who must travel to another country with an enemy.

Psalm 126
This psalm is a prayer for protection of your home and family. It can also be prayed for protection from having a stillborn child.

Psalm 127
This psalm can be a prayer for protection from anything that would harm your baby.

Psalm 128
This psalm can be a prayer for a woman to have a safe delivery.

Psalm 129
Pray this psalm to ask God to reveal to you things that you cannot see.

Psalm 130
This psalm can be a prayer for healing of your eyes.

Psalm 131
Pray this psalm with someone who needs help controlling his temper.

Psalm 132
This psalm can be a prayer for continued success in your marriage relationship.

Psalm 133
Pray this psalm when you need more friends.

Psalm 134
This psalm is a prayer for protection in school, whatever grade level your child is.

Psalm 135
This psalm is a serious prayer for repentance.

Psalm 136
This psalm can be prayed for help in dealing with the loss of families, friends, or fortune.

Psalm 137
Pray this psalm for a clean heart, even while troubled by your enemies.

Psalm 138
This psalm can be prayed for a deeper measure of love, or for more friends.

Psalm 139
Pray this psalm to increase your love for your partner

Psalm 140
This psalm can be prayed for help to overcome hatred in your relationships.

Psalm 141
Pray this psalm for help to overcome fear.

Psalm 142-143
These psalms are a prayer for the light of the Holy Spirit in the midst of a difficult situation.

Psalm 144
This psalm can be prayed for the healing of a broken hand.

Psalm 145
Pray this psalm for help to overcome an evil spirit.

Psalm 146
This psalm can be prayed for healing if you have been cut by a knife or another tool or weapon.

Psalm 147
This psalm can be prayed for protection of your house against thieves.

Psalm 148-149
Pray this psalm to claim victory over your oppressors.

Psalm 150
This psalm is a prayer of thanks to God for our nation and our families.

Printed in the United States
By Bookmasters